Lightning Bolt Books™

Bot Battles

Lola Schaefer

Lerner Publications ◆ Minneapolis

Thank you, Jeff Rosen, Program Director - Engineering, Robotics, and Advanced Technologies at Georgia Institute of Technology, for your careful assistance with this book.

Lerner Publications Company
An imprint of Lerner Publishing Group, Inc.
241 First Avenue North
Minneapolis, MN 55401 USA

For reading levels and more information, look up this title at www.lernerbooks.com.

Main body text set in Billy Infant regular.
Typeface provided by SparkType.

Editor: Alison Lorenz, **Photo Editor:** Rebecca Higgins
Lerner team: Sue Marquis

Library of Congress Cataloging-in-Publication Data

Names: Schaefer, Lola M., 1950- author.
Title: Bot battles / Lola Schaefer.
Description: Minneapolis, MN : Lerner Publications Company, an imprint of Lerner Publishing Group, Inc., 2021 | Series: Lightning bolt books. Robotics | Includes bibliographical references and index. | Audience: Ages 6-9. | Audience: Grades 2-3. | Summary: "Which robot is the smartest, the fastest, or the strongest? Learn what robots can do, how engineers design robots, and how scientists and students put their cool creations to the test"—Provided by publisher.
Identifiers: LCCN 2019045747 (print) | LCCN 2019045748 (ebook) | ISBN 9781541596979 (library binding) | ISBN 9781728400419 (ebook)
Subjects: LCSH: Robotics—Competitions—Juvenile literature. | Robots—Juvenile literature.
Classification: LCC TJ211.2 .S33 2021 (print) | LCC TJ211.2 (ebook) | DDC 796.16—dc23

LC record available at https://lccn.loc.gov/2019045747
LC ebook record available at https://lccn.loc.gov/2019045748

Manufactured in the United States of America
1-47803-48243-12/20/2019

Table of Contents

Robots Compete

Two robots battle. Their arms push, and their wheels crash. The robots bump, hit, flip, and fall. Which one will win?

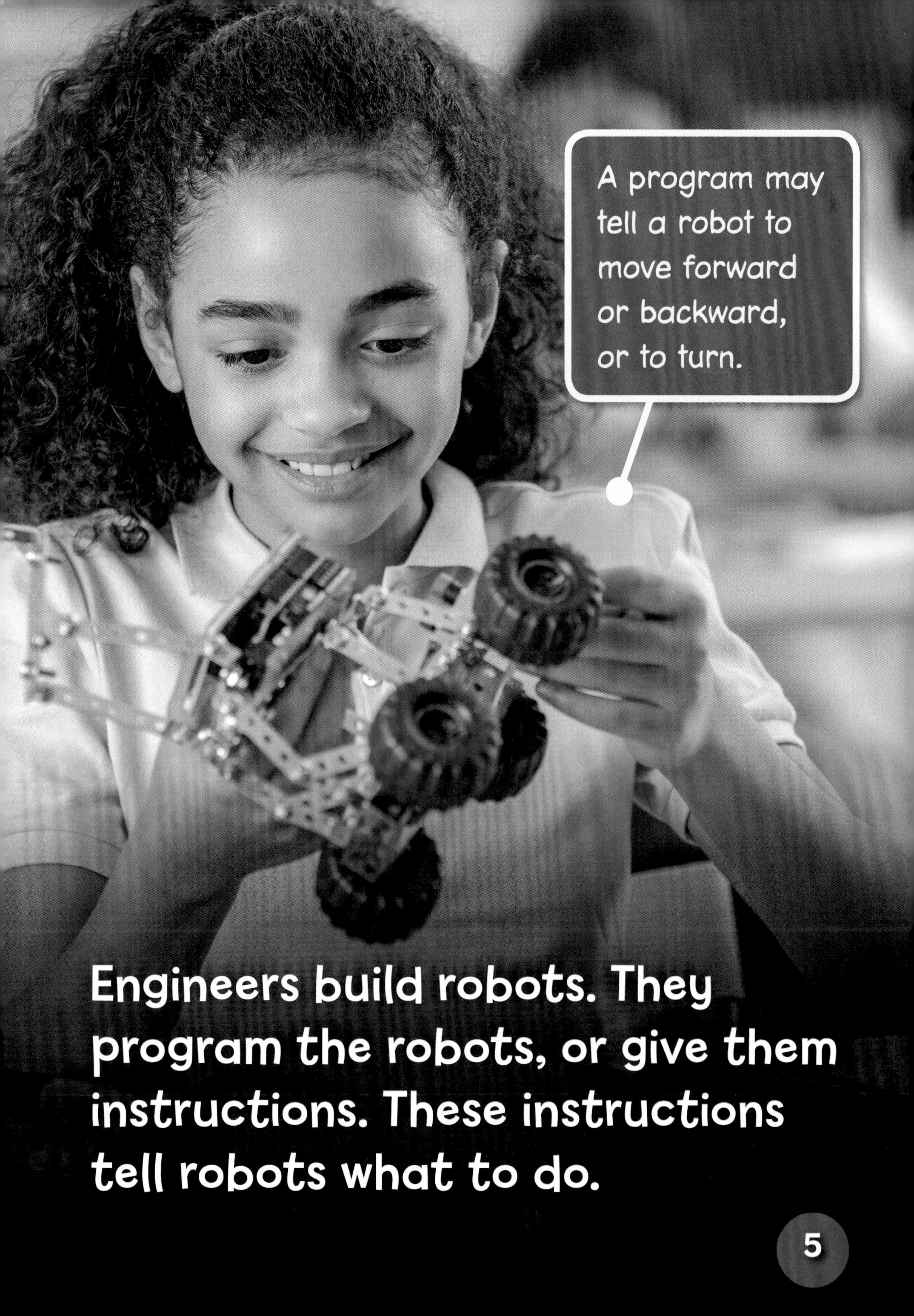

Engineers build robots. They program the robots, or give them instructions. These instructions tell robots what to do.

Some robots compete in contests. These robots need special skills to face off against other robots.

Contests often have robots grab objects and move them somewhere else.

Engineers fix robots' mistakes so the robots don't make them in competitions.

Engineers prepare for robot competitions. They test many programs to see which ones work best. They look for errors and correct them.

Smart, Fast, Strong

Some competitions give robots a challenge. Robots complete the challenge one step at a time. Each task is worth points. The robot with the most points wins.

In this contest, robots raced to fetch plastic cups and bring them to the finish line.

In other competitions, robots race. Engineers program robots to move quickly. The robots weigh very little. The fastest robot takes home a prize.

Some robots compete in games. They box or play soccer. These robots are strong. They can hit, run, and kick.

People want to build robot players that can compete against humans.

Sometimes engineers control their robots during a competition. Other robots are autonomous. This means they can move by themselves.

It Takes a Team

Students build robots for competitions too. Students form teams. They use math and science to create their robots. Some school teams use Lego bricks.

It's often useful to have many viewpoints tackling one challenge.

Each team member plays a different role. Together, they decide what their robot must do to complete the challenge. They program their robot with rules and commands.

Sometimes students work for months on one robot. They test it many times to make sure it works.

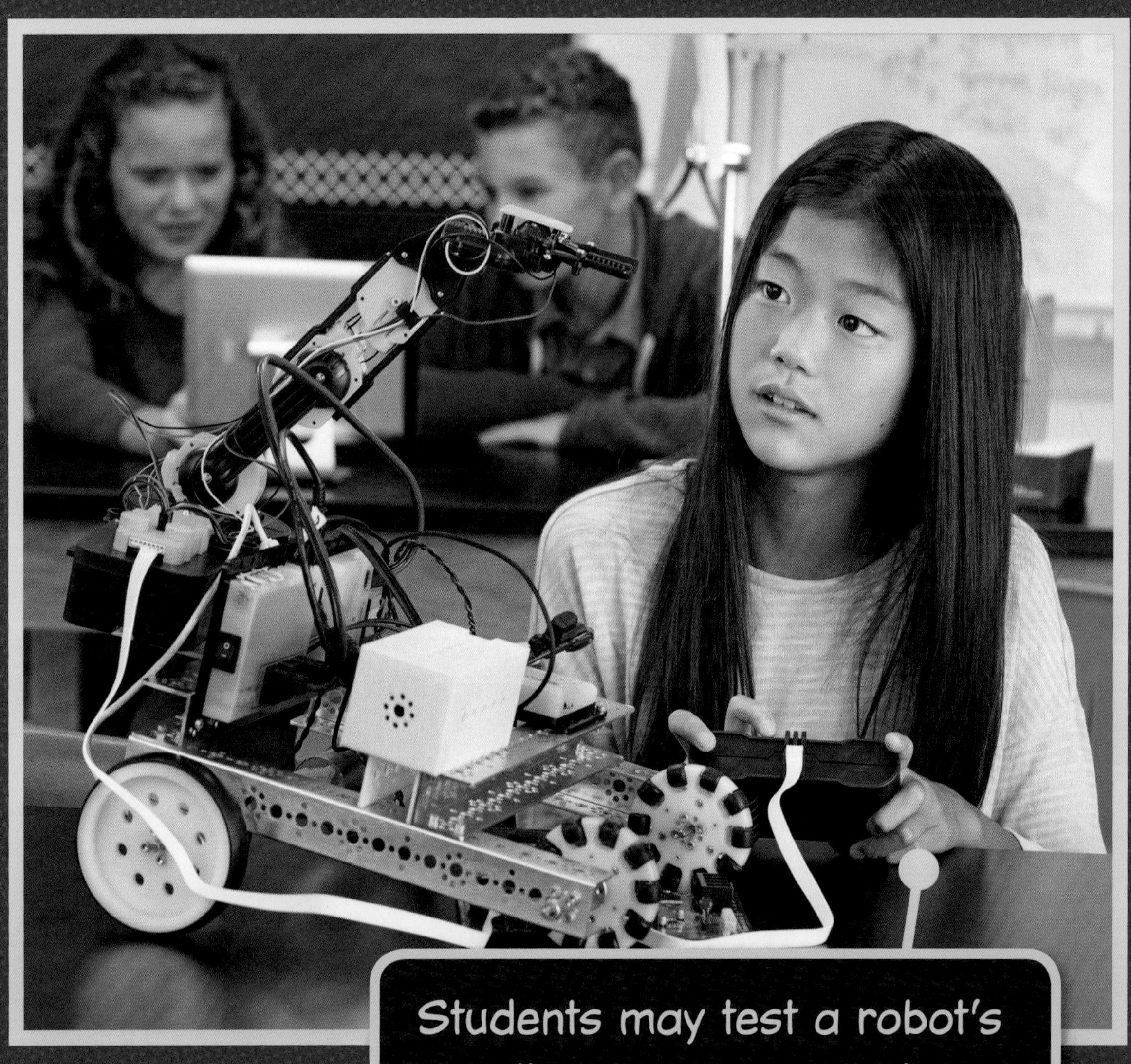

Students may test a robot's sturdiness or how well it follows directions.

This student came from Brazil to compete in Uruguay in 2019.

More than five hundred thousand students around the world compete in robot competitions. They meet new friends, gain skills, and have fun!

Robot Battles

In some competitions, two robots battle each other in an arena. The robot left standing is the winner.

These robots, Tombstone and Witch Doctor, competed on the TV show *BattleBots.*

The robots jab and ram each other. They push, slam, and crash together during three minutes of hard battle.

On the TV show *BattleBots*, engineers control their robots from outside the arena. They steer their robots away from saws and spikes that rise from the floor.

Robots battle behind thick glass so fans can't get hurt. Fans clap and cheer for their favorite robots!

Robot competitions can be exciting and fun!

Behind the Robot

Engineers design different robots for every competition. If the robot will be in a race, they work on creating the fastest legs or wheels. If the robot will pick up small items, the engineers design handlike grippers that can grab and hold. If the robot will need to lift, push, or carry, the engineers design armlike parts that are long and strong. Engineers test many parts to help their robots win.

Fun Facts

- The first successful autonomous car race took place in Spain in 2019.
- MegaBots are the largest fighting robots. A single robot can weigh up to 15 tons (13,608 kg).
- RoboCup holds robot soccer matches. The goal of this competition is to have a team of robots beat the human World Cup champions by 2050.
- Students compete in robot competitions in over one hundred countries.

Glossary

arena: a large area used for sports or entertainment

autonomous: able to run by itself, without help from a person

control: to make something or someone do what you want

engineer: someone trained to design and build machines

program: to enter step-by-step instructions into a computer or robot

skill: the learned ability to do something well

task: a piece of work to be done

Further Reading

FIRST Lego League Junior
https://www.firstinspires.org/robotics/flljr

Gagne, Tammy. *Robots*. Minneapolis: Cody Koala, 2019.

Latta, Sara L. *Zoom in on Educational Robots.* New York: Enslow, 2018.

Robot Facts for Kids
https://kids.kiddle.co/Robot

Schaefer, Lola. *Flying Robots.* Minneapolis: Lerner Publications, 2021.

Index

Photo Acknowledgments

Image credits: Matt Roberts/Getty Images, p. 2; MARK RALSTON/Getty Images, pp. 4, 16-18; SDI Productions/Getty Images, p. 5; Laura Lezza/Getty Images, p. 6; Prostock-Studio/Getty Images, p. 7; Anadolu Agency/Getty Images, p. 8; Paul Marotta/Getty Images, p. 9; KAZUHIRO NOGI/AFP/Getty Images, p. 10; Miguel Sotomayor/Getty Images, p. 11; https://www.gettyimages.com/detail/photo/kid-playing-with-his-drone-on-the-drone-royalty-free-image/636755326?adppopup=true, p. 12; monkeybusinessimages/Getty Images, p. 13; Ariel Skelley/Getty Images, p. 14; SOPA Images/Getty Images, p. 15; Anusak Laowilas/NurPhoto/Getty Images, p. 19; Jens Schlueter/Getty Images, p. 23.

Cover: MARK RALSTON/Getty Images.